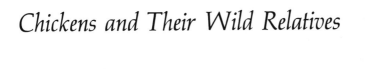

Chickens and Their Wild Relatives

Chickens
and
Their Wild Relatives

ALICE L. HOPF

Illustrated with photographs

DODD, MEAD & COMPANY · NEW YORK

1 2 3 4 5 6 7 8 9 10

Library of Congress Cataloging in Publication Data

Hopf, Alice Lightner, date
    Chickens and their wild relatives.

    Bibliography: p.
    Includes index.
    Summary: Discusses the physical
characteristics, behavior, and history of the
domestic chicken and its wild relatives,
including the grouse, pheasant, prairie chicken,
and ptarmigan.
    1. Galliformes—Juvenile literature.
2. Chickens—Juvenile literature. [1. Chickens.
2. Game and game birds. 3. Birds] I. Title.
QL696.G2H598 1982   598′.61   82-54385
ISBN 0-396-08085-5

For the Jessup Family of Goshen,
chicken breeders par excellence

Contents

Toy jug in the shape of a cock, with the Etruscan alphabet

1 How We Got Them

Chickens belong to a large group of birds called gallinaceous fowl. These are birds that find their food mostly on the ground and also nest on the ground, although some species may at times fly up into the trees. Most of them are medium-sized birds. Our chicken is considered typical of the group. It is believed to be descended from the jungle fowl of Asia, which have the scientific name of *Gallus gallus*. Gallinaceous birds are sometimes called "game birds," because so many of them, like the grouse, the pheasant, and the quail, are the favorite quarry of hunters.

The chicken is such a common domestic bird that it seems to have always been with us. Indeed, it was brought into our family of domestic animals during the period we call "prehistory"—sometime during the third millennium (3000 years) B.C. This was long before writing was invented.

It may seem that such a useful and succulent bird, just the right size for the oven or frying pan or regularly producing a bounty of eggs, should have been easily recognized as a welcome addition to the human larder. But this was not the case. Five thousand years ago, the chicken was a very different bird. Its ancestors, known as the red jungle fowl (*Gallus gallus*), are still living in the wilds of India and Southeast Asian countries, and they are about the size of our bantams (the smallest chickens). The unknown Dravidian villager, an early inhabitant of India, who first made a pet of a jungle cock, was not thinking of food. He was thinking of entertainment and probably of betting. For the first chickens were prized and domesticated because of the fighting abilities of the males.

The valley of the Indus River (now in Pakistan) sheltered one of the earliest agricultural civilizations of mankind. The two great cities, Mohenjo-Daro and Harappa, were each over three miles in circumference. The work of excavating and studying them began in the 1920s. This civilization dates back beyond 3000 B.C.

Archaeologists digging up the garbage dumps of ancient cities, and comparing the bones of animals found there, are confronted with the question: Was the animal killed in the hunt, or was it a domesticated creature, cared for by the people until it was needed for food? One way to tell the difference is by the size of the bones. Domestic animals are usually bigger than their wild ancestors. The femur (thigh bone) of a bird dug up at Mohenjo-Daro was 4 inches (103 mm.) long, whereas a similar bone from a wild bird is only 2.69 inches (69 mm.) long. The femur of a modern chicken, bred for the table, measures 4.48 inches (115 mm.).

10

This gives some idea of how an animal can change under domestication.

Today there are four species and numerous geographical breeds of the red jungle fowl. Other gallinaceous birds that people have tried to domesticate, such as peafowl and pheasants, have not changed from their wild ancestors as has the chicken and can hardly be considered domesticated.

When we look at the modern poultry industry, which has become big business today with the mass production of eggs and birds for the table, it is hard to realize that the chicken was not originally thought of as food. Apparently, those early people recognized an affinity between themselves and the aggressive, plucky little cocks, which would fly into a rage and fight to the death when their territory was invaded. Thus, cockfighting, and probably the betting that accompanies it, goes back to the dawn of history.

While the archaeologists found merely bones in the oldest layers of rock, in later deposits they dug up artistic representations. From the dig at Harappa come two clay figurines, one a cock and one a hen. And at Chanhu-Daro to the south, clay whistles were found shaped like small gallinaceous or chickenlike birds. However, as one of these is painted in vertical stripes, they may represent wild quail rather than tame chickens.

The very early Sumarian language has a word for cock, suggesting that the birds were soon carried along the trade routes from India to the early cities in the Tigris and Euphrates valleys.

And when the Aryans invaded India in the middle of the second millennium B.C., they quickly developed a liking for the colorful little cocks. The birds are mentioned in two of their epic poems, the *Atharv* and the *Yajur*, where the cock is praised for his courage and also as a herald of the dawn. Long before the invention of clocks and watches, or sundials and hourglasses, the rooster was valued for his dependable crowing at first light, an accomplishment that would long preserve him from the pot. Even today, in modern Turkey, cocks are bred for their crowing abilities and prizes are awarded for the cocks with the longest crow.

In time, these qualities led to the introduction of the chicken into religion. At a time when many people still worshipped animal gods, it is not surprising that the cock was given religious significance. And by 1000 B.C., they had become taboo as food in India. Other religions placed the cock among their gods. In that of Zoroaster, it appeared as the protector of good against evil, and the cock's waking crow at daybreak symbolized new light and life.

A painting of a cock was found in the tomb of Tutankhamen, showing that it was known in Egypt by 1350 B.C. However, chickens are mentioned in the annals of Thothmes III, about 100 years earlier, as the birds that lay eggs every day.

During the first millennium B.C., the domestic fowl spread throughout the ancient world. It was carried from Persia (a nation that was constantly conquering its neighbors and enlarging its borders) to the cities of Mesopotamia and Asia Minor and eventually to Greece. The Greeks called it the Persian bird and

Both sides of a classical coin, showing a cock and a hen

sometimes the Median bird (from the Persians and the Medes, ancient enemies of the Greeks), suggesting how they got the birds. Excavations in all these areas have produced seals and coins with representations of both the cock and the hen, showing that the birds were held in high esteem.

During the centuries of Greek and Roman civilization, the cock was a symbol of strength and bravery and was often presented as a gift to a boy or young man. There is a famous statue of the god Zeus, shown carrying off the youth Ganymede, who, according to legend, was so beautiful that the great god transported him to heaven to become the cup-bearer of the gods. While Zeus in the statue is carrying Ganymede, the boy on his part is carrying a cock.

The hen, on the other hand, became the symbol of fertility, because of the many eggs she lays. And in ancient Jewish ritual, both a cock and a hen were carried in the bridal procession.

Ancient religions not only dealt with the symbols of good and evil, but also with the problems of the future. Some of their most important functions were in omens and prophecies. The Romans seldom started an important activity without first determining the omens for its success. Animals were sacrificed and then cut up so that the priests could examine their entrails. However, transporting large animals for divination purposes, as might be needed for an army, posed problems. And war and battles are certainly times when omens and prophecy are much in demand. So the Romans invented a method called *oraculum ex tripudio*. This employed the use of chickens, which could easily be carried around by either the army or the navy. The hens were brought out in their cages, and grain was scattered in front of them. If the birds refused to eat, it was a bad omen and the battle should be postponed till the morrow. But if they ate well, it was a good sign and the troops immediately lined up to fight.

It is said that some generals starved their hens before a battle and then had them fed in front of the army so that the men could see how the gods were on their side. But, of course, there was always the chance that the priests might want to influence events by giving the hens a good feeding just before they were brought out for the demonstration. Such a situation developed just before the naval battle of Drepana during the first Punic War in 249 B.C. The birds were brought out on the flagship but refused to eat, and the consul, P. Claudius Pulcher, became incensed and threw them overboard, crying, "If they won't eat, let them drink!" Whether the birds had been overfed or were merely seasick is not recorded. But the consul was defeated in the battle, and the people of Rome laid the outcome to his disrespect of the gods and the omens.

In classical times, the use of chickens for food production increased, and the Romans developed the art of poultry raising into a science. They began to develop different strains of chickens by crossbreeding. A breed called the Adria, from Adria near Venice, was especially praised by writers of the time. White birds were generally frowned upon, as they were more easily seen and attacked by birds of prey. But they had their uses in religion, for the Egyptian god Anubis, whose worship was taken up by the Romans, demanded the sacrifice of white fowl.

During the Roman Empire, the art of cooking became highly developed and chickens were often on the menu. Books were written by such authors as Varro and Columella, telling the farmers how best to care for their birds. Hens should be fattened like geese, by hand-stuffing (having food stuffed down their throats). A waxing moon was the best time for hatching eggs, and an odd number of eggs should always be put under the hen. There were such suggestions as placing the chicken house near the kitchen so that the smoke from that area could blow among the hens and kill the lice.

Columella gave detailed directions about the best birds to select for breeding. His descriptions are remarkably similar to the "show points" used by farmers in Britain today. His works discuss housing and feeding, breeding and rearing, and the control of disease.

He even went into the problems of marketing, pointing out that only if the farmer lived near a city, with a market for young birds, should he set eggs for hatching late in the summer, as the chicks would not reach full growth before winter.

With the collapse of the Roman Empire, the art of poultry raising was neglected and lost. Not until the nineteenth century was the science again developed to such a peak. Then farmers went back to Columella to learn the art.

It is believed that the chicken was originally brought to Europe by two trade routes—across the Dardanelles to the Aegean (Greece) and through Scythia to the Teutons and Celts. Perhaps they first reached Italy, then Rome, from the north rather than the south, being traded down through Gaul, now France.

These theories are substantiated by various excavations. The earlier dates are based on bones. But excavations in Alsace and on the Upper Rhine show designs of cocks on belt buckles dating from 600 to 450 B.C. There is some argument about whether the designs really represent cocks. However, there is proof that the birds were being bred in Switzerland before 58 B.C. And they were definitely established in Britain before the Roman conquest, as Caesar states in his *De Bello Gallico*.

For a long time, it was taken for granted that the chicken was brought to the Americas shortly after the first voyage of Columbus. But now there is strong evidence that it was already here before he arrived. The scientist C. O. Sauer argues that the chicken was widespread over South America by the time the Spaniards arrived. Thus, while it has been supposed that Cabral, the Portuguese navigator and explorer, introduced it into Brazil in 1500, it was found in abundance by Magellan only 19 years later and 1,000 miles south of Cabral's landing point. In addition, the birds found by the Spanish explorers were quite different from the European stock. In some ways they resembled a breed we now call "Silkies," a very ancient breed, believed to have originated in China. Sauer also points out that the Indian tribes had their own name for the chicken, quite different from the Spanish word. He believes that they were brought to the Peruvian and Ecuadorian coasts from Asia during the ancient Chinese dynasties, when trade existed between the two continents.

The chicken arrived in China as a domestic bird by 1400 B.C. No doubt it came up through Southeast Asia from India. Or there may have been a separate domestication from wild birds in those areas. The Chinese birds are generally bigger and heavier than those of the West. This may be due to breeding or to a slightly different original ancestor. But that they all come from *Gallus gallus* is evident because even today Chinese birds can breed with our birds, and they have been used to create some of our larger and heavier chickens. Were they not the same species, they could not successfully interbreed.

With the decline of the Roman Empire and the beginning of the long period known as the Dark or Middle Ages, the chicken was demoted to become the scavenger of the barnyard. It had to live on whatever it could find for itself. It was of little value and was the food of the peasantry rather than the nobility. Most farms had a few, but not many, chickens and little was done in the way of caring for them or improving the breeds. It has been estimated that between 1333 and 1336, the number of birds on an estate varied from 7 to 49. In some areas where money was scarce, chickens were used to pay the rent, and the Channel Island of Guernsey paid tribute to the English kings with a poll tax of one pullet (a hen less than a year old) a year.

With time, the use of chickens for food increased and they were raised in greater numbers. In 1807, *The Complete Farmer or General Dictionary of Agriculture* was published. In this book, a suggestion was made that poultry farming should be run on a scientific basis, and the writer went back to the works of the Roman author Columella to find the proper methods. Six English breeds of chickens are mentioned: the Game, the White or English, the Black or Poland, the Darkling, the Large or Strakebag, and the Malay.

Later in the century, poultry shows and breeding societies became popular, paving the way for the modern methods of large-scale chicken farming with the production of high quality meat for the market and great numbers of eggs. The chicken had moved from its place in entertainment and religion to its position today as a major item of food for people.

2 Chickens Today

The nineteenth century saw the return of interest in the scientific breeding of chickens, but it took the twentieth century to turn plain chicken farming into big business. Instead of being just one aspect of farming, poultry raising has become a specialty. The big commercial farms concentrate on chickens and nothing else. The occupation has become an industry, where one farmer may concentrate on egg production and another will raise birds for the table. Even this is further broken down, some producers specializing in broilers (young birds) and others in roasters and capons.

Today, the small farmer does not have much of a chance in the commercial market, and many people who hoped to make a good living in the country raising chickens went broke and had to find other means of livelihood. Big growers have flocks numbering in the tens of thousands and, while it takes a lot of money to feed and manage such a flock, they can produce the eggs and meat at a much lower price than can the small farmer, and thus can undersell him in the market.

Another fairly recent development is the mechanization of chicken farming. Birds used to be kept out of doors for a good part of the time, and were brought in at night for safety. In some instances, this is still the practice. And even when the birds are kept entirely indoors, in large barnlike buildings, they are allowed to run free. In such cases, constant cleaning of the houses is required and frequent feeding, watering, and collecting of eggs. All this demands a great deal of labor, either by the owner or by his workers. In the mechanized system, such work is cut to a minimum and the producer saves money on labor.

In this method, the birds are kept in wire cages. They even stand on wire. Their excrement falls through the mesh into a pit or onto boards, where it is collected and sold for manure. The food and water troughs are on the outside of the cages, and the birds poke their heads through the holes in the wire mesh to eat and drink. The troughs are automatically refilled. The cages are tilted slightly so that as soon as an egg is laid it rolls out of the cage and onto a tray where it is collected either by hand or on a moving belt. Since the cages are all indoors, they are artificially lighted and the length of day and amount of light the birds receive can be carefully controlled. Some birds are kept constantly in the light, so that they will continue the eating-laying cycle at a peak, and when they have passed that mark, they are replaced with new birds. In such a mechanized system, one person can care for as

USDA Photo by William E. Carnahan

Egg gathering at Hurst Egg Farm in Chesterfield, South Carolina

many as 10,000 laying hens or 20,000 birds being raised for food.

The Romans did not favor white birds, because they were an easy target for birds of prey and their bows and arrows could not reach as high as a circling hawk. But today we have the rifle to take care of that problem, and birds that are kept indoors their entire lives do not face the hazard. One of the most popular breeds for egg production is the all-white Leghorn. Leghorns lay white

21

eggs, which are often preferred in the market. A good laying hen can produce 19 to 20 dozen eggs during the year.

Other breeds, such as Rhode Island Reds, Plymouth Rocks, New Hampshires, and Wyandottes, are popular. The larger, heavier kinds, such as Plymouth Rocks and Rhode Island Reds, are raised to be sold as meat for the table. Much scientific work has been done on crossbreeding to produce the best chickens for these different roles.

In addition to the standard commercial breeds with their various crosses, breeders have produced a number of exotic species, specializing in ornate plumage rather than in their qualities as food producers. These are ornamental birds, raised for exhibition in poultry shows. They range from the bantams, weighing only 20 ounces (567 grams), to the Brahmas, which may weigh 12 pounds (5½ kilograms). Birds designed for cockfighting and breeds originating in the Mediterranean area have long legs. Breeds like the Cochin, brought originally from China, are large, heavy birds with short legs, feathered all the way down to the toes. Much attention is paid to the color and mottling of the feathers, which may be red, buff, white, black, or speckled. One breed, called the Black Polish, has a striking white crest that almost covers the eyes. All these breeds have been developed by specialists over years of careful interbreeding.

There is also great variety in the combs, especially in the males. Some are very large and droop down over the head. The Sicilian Buttercups and the Augsburgers have a double cuplike comb.

Then there are the Tailless chickens and the Bearded fowl, having a growth of feathers around the face and beak. There are the Frizzled chickens and the Japanese Silk fowl, which have feathers suggestive of their names. And in East Asia, selective breeding has produced the Long-tailed fowl, whose tail feathers achieve astonishing lengths.

The incubator for artificial brooding of eggs was invented by the ancient Egyptians, who built special ovens for that purpose. Today we have mechanically controlled, electrical incubators, where the eggs are kept at just the right temperature and humidity. Eggs can also be mechanically turned, although some farmers do that job themselves. They must be turned at least four times a day, so that the chick inside will not stick to the shell. In nature, the setting hen does this, but sometimes she breaks the eggs in the process. The incubator eliminates the mistakes of an awkward bird. It also can take care of a great many more eggs than can a single hen. A hen can cover from 9 to 15 eggs, depending on her size. But she has to get up and go out to eat and drink and some hens even get bored and quit. The incubator solves all these problems. Some firms make a business of raising chicks by incubator. Many farmers start their flocks from baby chicks, bought from such establishments. But others have their own incubators and buy fertile eggs from companies that specialize in them. Eggs sold for the table are not fertile. The hens never see a rooster. To get fertile eggs, the farmer must have roosters with his hens. A flock of 100 pullets needs six to eight males to ensure that the eggs will

USDA *Photo by George A. Robinson*

A batch of 30,000 day-old chicks are headed for a farm from McCarty-State Pride Hatchery.

Broiler grower Maurice Layton checks the feeders in one of his poultry houses where in a few weeks time these 15,000 baby chicks will grow into four-pound broilers.

be fertile. A producer who goes into this line of the business should know something about genetics so that he will produce satisfactory eggs and strong young birds for his customers.

Something the ancient Romans did not have was modern medicine. When their birds got sick, they had little science and few weapons with which to fight the disease. And there are a great many diseases that afflict chickens. This was still the situation when farmers began the serious breeding of the birds in the nineteenth century. But with the twentieth century, the science of medicine began a swift climb upwards, and with the discovery of penicillin and other antibiotics in mid-century, the control of many diseases was assured. The benefits of human medicine were quickly passed on to veterinary medicine, including the care of chickens.

It is generally agreed that preventing the outbreak of disease is easier than stopping it once it has begun. Consequently, vaccination is in order for large flocks of birds. One of the most devastating diseases of the past, Newcastle disease, is now controlled by vaccination. Also laryngotracheitis, fowl pox, and cholera are prevented in this way. In some cases, the chicks are treated early in life. Vaccination for Marek's disease is usually done when they are only a day old. Commercial breeders who buy young chicks expect them to have been immunized for some of these diseases.

The control of disease in chickens and their general health problems are monitored from Washington and also helped locally by the states. The Department of Agriculture publishes reports and bulletins about the industry and the National Poultry Improvement Plan does blood tests for disease on the flocks of its members. Thus stock bought from this group is usually disease free. Proper feeding of the birds also helps to keep them healthy. Science has determined their nutritional requirements, and vitamins, trace elements, and amino acids are added to commercial chicken feed.

Even healthy birds can get into a lot of trouble simply by their behavior. Like most birds that live in flocks, chickens set up a pecking order. In fact, it was with chickens that the behavior was first observed and studied, and it has since been found in wild birds, in cattle and deer, and in wolves and lions. Chickens peck each other as a way of determining rank in the group. This behavior can start when chicks are only a few weeks old, and sometimes it is carried over into serious attacks. If blood is drawn, the whole flock may peck an individual to death. To prevent what starts out as feather picking and may end up as cannibalism, various methods have been tried. Sometimes just giving the birds more room or different feed and water may do the trick. Sometimes the application of antipick ointments helps. If none of this stops the attacks, the birds may have to be "debeaked." About half of the beak is cut off, leaving the upper beak shorter than the lower. The chickens can eat, but cannot hurt each other. Some breeders want their baby chicks to be debeaked, but in that case the beaks grow back again. There are debeaking machines on the market with an electrically heated blade that cuts and cauterizes at the same time, thus avoiding bleeding.

Chickens are very much creatures of habit. Any sudden change in the environment or their feed can put them off laying. Any change in the person who cares for them, or even in his or her clothing, can cause panic in the flock. In order to prevent losses, they must be handled with care.

Since the domestic chicken is descended from the jungle fowl, we can expect to find their general behavior quite similar. Of the four wild species living today, only one is monogamous—the green jungle fowl. All the others, like our chickens, are polygamous, one

27

cock accumulating three to five hens that he mates with and defends, even helping them to find suitable nesting spots. The hens lay from five to nine eggs, which vary in color from white to a reddish cream. The baby down of the chicks soon changes to feathers and, by the time the chicks are eight days old, they can fly from branch to branch and roost with their parents in the trees.

Jungle fowl, like our chickens, enjoy a dust bath to rid themselves of parasitic insects but seldom go into the water and look for a sheltered spot when it rains. They start feeding at first light and go to roost in the trees as soon as the sun sets, a habit that is being disrupted in domestic fowl by the use of artificial light. Probably this well-known preference accounts for our expression, "to go to bed with the chickens."

Our chickens and their wild ancestors have a variety of sounds for communication. Most people are familiar with the cock's crow and the hen's cackle upon laying an egg. She also has special little calls for bringing her chicks together and a different sound for warning against danger. Even before they are hatched, the chicks chirp to their mother from inside the egg, and after hatching they warble as they settle down under her protective feathers. The cock, too, has an alarm signal and a special gobble for talking with his hens.

Three of the species of jungle fowl can interbreed, and most of them may have donated some genes to the domestic chicken. They include the red jungle fowl (*Gallus gallus*), Sonnerat's jungle fowl (*Gallus sonnerati*), and LaFayette's jungle fowl (*Gallus lafayettii*). The fourth, the green jungle fowl (*Gallus varius*), is said to be the most beautiful and most divergent. It is the only one that cannot interbreed with the domestic chicken. The cocks have a smooth-edge comb and only one wattle (the bare, fleshy skin on the bird's face) and their crowing is said to be shrill.

3 Grouse

America is rich in wild gallinaceous fowl, and perhaps the best known is the grouse. These are brown birds, mottled in various shades of tan and gray, with yellow or red markings in their feathers. They have a variety of popular names, most given to them by the first colonists who met them as the settlements moved westward. Grouse are northern birds, found in all lands north of latitude 26°, which passes through Mexico and the tip of Florida. Their nostrils are hidden by feathers and the hind toe is somewhat higher than the other three. Most species have feathers around the lower legs (tarsi) and they are without spurs.

Grouse live mostly on the ground, although some of them can fly quite well. They walk about, pecking in the grass and ground cover to find their food. Some live in forests and some in open prairies. Some are solitary birds and some live in groups. All of them build carefully hidden nests on the ground. Grouse are masters of camouflage. Nests are hard to find, and once the chicks are hatched they can seemingly vanish from sight at the alarm call of the hen and may easily be stepped on by a searcher. The adult birds eat a variety of vegetation and fruits. Chicks run after insects. In winter they eat buds and catkins and even the needles of fir trees.

The most famous American grouse is the ruffed grouse (*Bonasa umbellus*). Its range covers most of the United States and north into Canada and even Alaska, as far as there are trees. But since, like all grouse, it is a good bird to eat, it has been exterminated by hunters from such states as Iowa, Nebraska, Kansas, Missouri, and Arkansas. It is usually thought of as a northeastern bird, perhaps because the early settlers in that area were impressed and mystified by its "drumming," and naturalists and woodsmen frequently wrote of it.

The ruffed grouse gets its name from a ruff of feathers around its neck which it can turn upwards when in fighting stance. In such displays, it also erects the tail feathers into a fan that is tilted forward. It is a brown bird, about the size of a bantam, and its feathers are mottled with various shadings of red, lighter brown, and gray. The bird's plumage depends on its age and sex and on the part of the country where it lives. Those in the north have gray tails, whereas in Pennsylvania, the grays, called silvertails, are rare. In the western birds, redtails are rare. Birds with copper-colored ruffs, called "red ruffs," turn up throughout the range.

The ruffed grouse live and eat like most grouse everywhere. Their food is chiefly vegetable, except for the chicks, which eat a

Ruffed grouse

lot of insects. The adults eat all kinds of buds and berries, seeds and grasses, and nuts of all kinds. Fruits such as rose hips, grapes, and wild berries are favored. In the winter, when the ground is covered with snow, they fly up into the trees and find early buds. Farmers have accused them of attacking the buds on apple trees, but scientists have found that this pruning is good for the trees and promotes a better crop. Grouse also eat the berries of poison ivy without harm to themselves, but people have been poisoned by eating the flesh of such birds.

32

The hen does all the work of building the nest—a simple scrape in the leaves or dirt—and raising the young. But her nest is well camouflaged and she defends her 9 to 28 eggs energetically. She seldom flushes till the intruder is almost upon her, and then she flies up with such a whirring of wings that the surrounding leaves are blown over the eggs. She then sits in a nearby tree until the danger is past. When the chicks hatch, she broods them under her feathers against the damp and cold and leads them to the best spots to find food. At her call, they freeze into immobility and stay that way until she signals that all is safe. They are so hard to see that a hunter can easily step on one and crush it.

The cock spends the springtime defending his territory and

Female ruffed grouse on nest, incubating eleven eggs

USDA Photo by Dr. Alfred O. Gross

displaying to his hens. He usually has only one, but if another comes into his territory, he will mate with her, too. Grouse are polygamous and do not mate for life. He selects one or more drumming logs or rocks, where he struts and postures and makes the peculiar drumming sound for which this species is famous. From early spring, this sound can be heard in the woods. Usually his special log is an old one, large and moss-covered. It is not necessarily in the center of his territory, which may be no more than a quarter of a mile in circumference. Usually he selects a spot in a forest of hardwoods, because the trees will still be bare and he can see all around to watch for enemies. At the same time, he likes a few bushes nearby where he can hide, coming out when he feels like it to drum on his log. The ruffed grouse is a nonmigratory species. Winter and summer, he seldom strays far from home.

From the earliest colonial times, there was much argument about how the ruffed grouse makes his drumming sound. This can be heard a quarter of a mile away, but the sound is deceptive and birds that seem to be at a distance may be quite close by. The sound can resemble that of a man sawing. The Indians called him the carpenter bird, believing that he beat the log with his wings. Other early naturalists claimed that the bird beat his wings against his sides or against each other. Not until the invention of the high-speed movie camera was the matter settled. In the spring of 1929, a bird near Ithaca, New York, was photographed with fast film, which proved that as the wings strike the air in an outward and upward motion, they produce this sound—a kind of sonic boom.

USDA—SCS Photo by L. D. Rezek

Grouse drumming, South Dakota

Although other birds make noises with their wings, none of them has this power and effectiveness.

There are many comic stories told about the ruffed grouse. When spring comes, the cocks are completely immersed in their display behavior and, of course, rush to attack any other male that answers their signals or comes into their territory. They are prone to take umbrage with human sounds which are similar to their drumming. Thus the sound of a tractor will bring forth an answer from a displaying cock. The birds have been known to follow a tractor around the field as it prepares for spring planting. In some cases, the cock appeared friendly and to be attracted by the noise.

In other instances, the bird rushed to attack the machine and even the man driving it.

The same effect has been noted by woodcutters. The sounds of their axes hitting the trees must sound to the grouse cock like the drumming of a rival. Leonard Lee Rue III, in his book *The World of the Ruffed Grouse*, tells the story of Jonah Howell, who worked in a New Jersey State Forest. One day he was making holes in the earth around an old apple tree to apply fertilizer, when the thumping sound he made attracted a male grouse. He found himself being attacked by the cock. But since he did not fight back, the bird apparently decided that it had won the battle. After that he seemed to adopt Jonah. Every day he turned up where the man was working and soon became friendly enough to be hand-fed and even picked up. Sam, as the grouse was called, became famous and a great attraction for visitors and campers at the park. He came readily to be fed, but only Jonah could pick him up.

The gray or blue grouse (*Dendragapus obscurus*) is found in our mountainous western states, from Arizona and New Mexico to Colorado. They are dusky birds that live in forests from the foothills to timberline. The bird has a small, pointed head and a compact body, and prefers to live in deep pine forests. The nest, with seven to ten eggs, is often hidden in the grass of a clearing and the hen may sometimes be found taking a dustbath in the sand of a woodland trail.

During the mating season, the cock struts about, inflating his two reddish neck pouches and hooting in a loud voice that seems

36

Female blue grouse on nest

to come from all directions and can be heard from afar. Often he displays on foot, spreading his tail feathers, which are tipped forward, while his head is pulled in and back and his wings drag on the ground. At other times, he calls as he flies from tree to tree.

Farther north in the Rockies—Idaho, Wyoming, eastern Oregon, and north into Canada—is the range of Richardson's grouse (*Dendragapus obscurus richardsoni*). The species are differentiated by the tail feathers. The blue grouse has a dark gray band across the end of its tail feathers, which is lacking in Richardson's grouse. The two species have much the same habits and behavior. While

37

the mating display is similar, Richardson's grouse gives a much softer call. Its hooting can hardly be heard from 75 yards away. It also makes a fluttering sound, achieved by falling out of a tree and tumbling over as he comes to earth. Once the ground is reached, he runs at the female and hoots.

Still farther west, along the coast of California and Oregon and up into Canada and Alaska, we find the sooty grouse (*Dendragapus fuliginosus*). These are all very similar birds and are identified by their general coloring and the designs on their tail feathers. The males display by hooting and strutting about, while the females build the nests and raise the young. The chicks are able to run about and begin feeding themselves soon after hatching and are well trained by the hen to freeze into invisibility at her special call. The female cackles much like the domestic hen. At night, these grouse fly up into the tops of tall fir trees, often from 12 to 30 feet (3 to 9 meters) above the ground. There they roost in a thick mat of branches, about eight feet out from the trunk, where their sooty coloring blends well with the mossy branches and they are concealed by the overhang.

There are several subspecies of the sooty grouse, including the Sierra grouse (*Dendragapus fuliginosus sierrae*), found in the coastal mountains of the Sierra Nevada, from southern Washington into California; the Mount Pinos grouse (*Dendragapus fuliginosus howardi*), in southern California's Kern County; and the Sitka grouse (*Dendragapus fuliginosus sitkensis*), peculiar to some islands off southeastern Alaska. The Sierra grouse like to do their courting from the tops of tall pine trees, often 60 feet above the ground. The cocks stand on high branches close to the trunks for hours and periodically utter their loud hooting. In the Sitka grouse, the females have a distinctive reddish coloring. On the whole, this group of western grouse have very similar behavior.

In our eastern states, we have the Hudsonian spruce grouse (*Canachites canadensis*). This bird is seldom found far from the wilderness. Unlike its cousin, the ruffed grouse, it has never learned to distrust humans. It has been given the popular name of "fool hen" because it will let a hunter approach close enough to catch it with a noosed pole or a thrown rock. So while it seemingly has no objection to living close to settlements, the individuals that do so are soon killed off and only the wilderness population remains.

The spruce grouse likes dense marshes and tangles of spruce

Spruce grouse

forest. It feeds on the buds, tips, and needles of spruce and also favors a fir and larch diet. Like the western grouse, the hen makes only a shallow depression in the mossy ground, which she lines with leaves and grass. She lays 10 to 12 eggs, which are said to be the prettiest of all grouse eggs. The colors range from cinnamon to pink or creamy buff, boldly marked with spots of dark or light brown.

This eastern grouse uses wing-drumming in its courtship, but not to such an extent as the famous ruffed grouse. It seems to have improved upon the fluttering sounds produced by Richardson's grouse when tumbling from a tree, but not to have developed the act to the extent of that practiced by the ruffed grouse. The cock likes to take a stand between two trees some 20 feet apart and with long lower branches. Standing on one of these branches, he allows himself to fall downward. Then beating and fluttering his wings, he flies up into the other tree. Presently, he repeats this ritual, and thus swings from tree to tree, all the while making the fluttering sound with his wings. If two such proper trees are not available, the cock will find an open spot and, standing in the center, jump periodically into the air, fluttering his wings as he comes down.

These actions do produce a slight drumming sound, though not nearly as spectacular as that of the ruffed grouse. It can be heard at any time of the year and is not peculiar to the courting and nesting season. Unlike the ruffed grouse, the spruce grouse does not object to an audience. While great stealth must be used to view a ruffed grouse drumming, the spruce grouse will merely peer curi-

© Leonard Lee Rue III

Male greater prairie chicken "dancing"

ously at an observer and then go on with his act. This is quite in character for a bird that has been dubbed "fool hen."

In the central part of the United States and Canada lives a somewhat different relative of the chicken. Known as prairie chickens, they are species of grouse living in the vast treeless plains. Three species are recognized. The greater prairie chicken (*Tympanuchus cupido*) has the most extensive range. It is found

41

from Saskatchewan in Canada southward to Minnesota, Wisconsin, and Michigan, and even as far south as Louisiana and Texas. Attwater's prairie chicken (*Tympanuchus cupido attwateri*) is a smaller, darker bird, found only in southwestern Louisiana and eastern Texas. And the lesser prairie chicken (*Tympanuchus pallidicinctus*) inhabits the Great Plains region in Colorado and Kansas south to Texas and possibly into southeastern New Mexico. Although the lesser prairie chicken is much smaller than the greater, it is said to be full of spirit and energy.

Prairie chickens eat more grain than their cousins, the grouse, but otherwise their life-style is much the same. However, there is a marked difference in the courting procedures of the cocks. While grouse are individualists, each cock setting up his own territory and display stand, the prairie chickens go through the ritual of courting in a group.

A small group of males may use the same area in successive seasons, a half dozen or so arriving in the spring and putting on their display dances day after day. Birds stand some ten yards apart and utter their crowing or booming sounds, which are part challenge to the other cocks and part call for the females. The whole ritual may seem hilarious to a human observer, but it is deadly serious to the birds. The act begins with the male doing a little dance, its feet striking the earth so fast that a rolling sound is produced. Then the cock inflates the big orange air sacs on either side of his neck. His tail is spread out and held straight up, his wings droop, and the feathers of his neck rise up. Looking quite ferocious

Male lesser prairie chicken booming

for a chicken, he jerks out his booming calls, which are punctuated as the air sacs become deflated. As though excited by this effort, the cock then jumps into the air, whirls around and struts a defiance to his neighbors.

When a female arrives at the display station, battle is joined by the males. They rush at each other, with necks extended and tails erect, and the amount of feathers left on the ground is evidence of the intensity of the battle. Eventually, each cock manages to corral a watching hen and lead her away from the arena, and mating and nesting begin.

There was once another species similar to the prairie chickens

43

White-tailed ptarmigan

© *Charles G. Summers, Jr., c/o Leonard Rue Enterprises*

that inhabited the eastern seaboard of the United States. The heath hen (*Tympanuchus cupido cupido*) was hunted so extensively and its habitat became so restricted by human settlements that it has become extinct. The last heath hen died on Martha's Vineyard Island early in this century.

The ptarmigan is the grouse of the Far North. Its range is circumpolar, and it is found in all lands around the Arctic Circle. Thus, similar birds inhabit not only North America, but Europe and Asia as well. Different peoples have given it different names, but it is basically the same bird.

The chief difference between the ptarmigan and the more

44

southerly grouse is that its legs are completely feathered and the toe feathers act like snowshoes so that the bird can walk across deep snow. It is also unusual in that it changes color with the seasons. In winter the bird is all white so that it can hide from predators in the snow. As spring advances, the white feathers are shed and darker ones take their place, providing camouflage against the part-snow, part-rock landscape. The ptarmigan has few trees or bushes to hide in, as it lives above the northern treeline.

The willow ptarmigan (*Lagopus lagopus albus*) breeds in Can-

Willow ptarmigan changing to winter white

ada and Alaska, as far north as Point Barrow and Nome, northern Quebec and Newfoundland. In winter, the birds move south, but theirs is not such an all-out migration as with most birds. Their southward movements depend upon the weather, the amount of snow, and the availability of food.

Like other grouse, ptarmigan eat leaves and buds of trees, such as willows, birches, alders, as well as wild berries. (In the Far North, trees are more like shrubs.) In winter they subsist on the twigs of such shrubs. They also eat any insects they can find. Their nests are similar to those of other grouse. In courting, the males strut and display their feathers. Their calling is closer to that of the Canada grouse. They do not have the booming or drumming of the birds of the south, but content themselves with jumping into the air. At the top of an especially high jump, the male soars aloft and then descends in a spiral to his original point, at the same time crying his challenge and vibrating his wings. The finale is always a battle between the males, making the feathers fly.

Once these battles have been decided, the birds form pairs. The cock stays with the female during nesting, often making a little nest for himself nearby, where he can watch over her safety. In 1927, Joseph Dixon described such a protective male ptarmigan. In that area, short-billed gulls make a practice of attacking nesting ptarmigans and stealing their eggs. They fly at the hen in a well-organized group. While one tries to make her shift about on the nest, the others rush in to grab an exposed egg. When the gulls appear, the hen gives her special cry for help and the cock rushes out of his hiding place and attacks the marauders. He flies right into them, knocking them down with his onslaught. Since the ptarmigan weighs about a third more than a gull, his attack is usually successful.

There are a number of species and subspecies of ptarmigan in the land surrounding the North Pole. Another well-known one is the rock ptarmigan (*Lagopus rupestris*). This bird, which frequents even more desolate country than the willow ptarmigan, ranges from Alaska and the Aleutian Islands through northern Canada and Newfoundland to Greenland. They fly rapidly and make extensive migrations about their range as the seasons change.

Female rock ptarmigan and young

They move in flocks and are well camouflaged by their changing plumage to match the changes in ground cover. They are pure white during the winter snows and molt to darker shades as the snow melts.

The life of the rock ptarmigan is similar to that of other grouse and ptarmigan, but there is a difference in the courtship. Instead of flying into the air, like the willow ptarmigan, this cock runs in circles around his chosen mate. His tail is spread, his wings drag along the ground, and his head and neck are stretched out as far as possible while every feather seems to stand on end. Making a peculiar growling noise, he twists his body and jumps into the air. If another male is present, this display is directed at him and a violent fight ensues. A wiley maneuver has been observed among the birds in which the apparent loser runs away and, while he is being chased, suddenly flies back to the female, arriving there before the supposed victor.

The cock is very devoted to his mate, staying with her during the nesting period and sometimes flying between her and the hunter in an effort to draw the enemy away.

In Europe, the grouse is known as the capercaillie (*Tetrao urogallus*). It is much like our ruffed grouse, only larger. It is the biggest of the grouse, the cock measuring 43.3 inches (110 cm.) and weighing 8 to 13 pounds (4 to 6 kg.). He has bright shades of green and blue in his neck feathers and some red feathers over the eyes. Hens are smaller, their brown and black feathers marked with white.

Originally they ranged all across northwestern Europe and

northern Asia, but hunting has exterminated them from much of their range. Like their American cousins, they dine on twigs, buds, and berries, and in winter on the needles of pine, spruce, and fir trees. The chicks need protein and eat a lot of insects and snails. This species is hard to raise in captivity as the baby birds are subject to diseases and vulnerable to damp and cold. One zoologist kept the last chick of a brood in his room, where it slept at the foot of his bed. If left alone, it would peep "*dee-dee*"—the grouse lost call.

Like our ruffed grouse, the capercaillie cock defends his displaying ground and territory where he sometimes attacks animals and humans as rivals. He offers little help to the hen in raising the chicks. The eggs are the size of chicken eggs and the hen lays six to ten in her nest.

Another Old World species of grouse is the black grouse (*Lyru-*

Black grouse

rus tetrix), which is found all across northern Europe and Asia. The courting display of this grouse is said to be the inspiration for the famous Bavarian Schuhplattler peasant dance. When dancing, the men jump wildly about, slapping the ground and their knees in imitation of the bird's wing-beating. The girls, like the quiet little hens, do nothing but a slow rotation in one spot. They are picked up by the men and thrown and whirled about. Today the black grouse, like so many of its relatives, is declining in numbers.

The Asian relative of the black grouse, the Caucasian black grouse (*Lyrurus mlokosiewiczi*), has a similar life-style but lives in forested mountains from 4,500 to 9,000 feet high (1,372.5 to 2,745 meters). They like alpine meadows and thickets of rhododendron and dwarf birch. In winter, they bury themselves in the snow. The cocks congregate on a special mating ground, but their displays are not as prolonged and violent as those of their European relatives.

4 Quail

Quail are among the smallest of the chickenlike birds. They are brown, short-tailed birds and have no spurs. Probably the best known is the eastern bobwhite (*Colinus virginianus*). Throughout the woods of the eastern United States, you can hear his voice in spring and summer. Even though you cannot see the bird, there's no mistaking his call, for it sounds exactly like his name: *"Bob-white! Bob-white!"* Originally a native of the eastern seaboard states, this little quail likes to live around farmlands, and as the original colonists spread westward, the bird followed along, so that now they are found throughout the Middle West and as far as eastern Texas, Colorado, and the Dakotas.

The bobwhite is one of the most helpful and beneficial birds for the farmer. Foraging through and around the fields, they eat quantities of destructive insects, including potato beetles, aphids, and grasshoppers. They also devour a variety of weed seeds, an-

Male bobwhite quail

other boon to the farmer. Any grain they may eat is that left over in the fields after harvesting.

As with most chickenlike birds, the bobwhites stay in flocks or coveys during the winter. They huddle together against the cold and have been known to dive into a snowbank for protection, for snow is a warming blanket for both plants and animals. When spring comes, the covey breaks up and it is then that we hear the cheery *bob-white!* call. This is the cock's challenge to other males in the neighborhood, as he establishes and patrols his territory. The hen has a soft, clear call and when she answers, the cock flies to her and struts about, displaying in front of her. Often he has to

52

chase her, both birds running about through the grass and thickets, the hen always managing to keep some five feet ahead of her admirer.

If another cock turns up to dispute the territory and the possession of the hen, a fight will take place, the two males going at each other as vigorously as any fighting cocks. In fact, dead cock quail have been found in the wild with the flesh bitten off around the head and neck, showing how serious these battles can be.

After the pair of quail has mated, it may be two weeks to a month before nesting begins, depending on the weather. The two stick together faithfully, following each other around in the continuous search for food. Usually the hen is in the lead, with the cock keeping close behind her. He is very attentive, even offering her the insects he has caught. Observers have seen a cock, after a lively chase, hold up a grasshopper in his beak and give a soft *cu-cu-cu* to alert the hen. When she hurried over to him, he gave her the insect.

Like other gallinacious birds, the quail's nest is a simple affair, but extremely well concealed. People tell of weeding their garden within a few feet of a quail's nest, quite unaware that the birds were there. A study of 602 quail nests, made in 1931, found that 97 were in woods, 336 in broomsedge fields, 88 in fallow fields, and a few in cultivated fields.

The quail hen finds a spot among thick vegetation and scoops out a shallow hole which she lines with leaves and grass. Then she weaves together the grass or other vegetation from either side into a kind of arch, leaving only a small opening through which she can come and go and survey the surroundings as she sits upon her nest. Any vines or briers near the nest are woven into the arch, making an impenetrable cover and concealment. Often the male takes part in building the nest, and one observer, writing in the last century, tells of finding such a structure because the cock kept whistling as he worked, thus leading the observer to the spot.

The hen quail is a good layer and anywhere from 12 to 20 eggs have been found in her nest. Nests with as many as 30 or 37 eggs are presumed to be the work of two hens. Bobwhites have been known to lay their eggs in the nests of other birds. One report from 1897 tells of a quail's egg in a towhee's nest, and another mentions a meadowlark's nest with five eggs of the lark and four of the quail. In another report, a quail's nest was found with 12 quail eggs and two from a domestic hen. During the incubation period of 23 days, the cock helps out. In 1931, a study was made of quail nests in Georgia and Florida and 73 were found with the cock sitting, 175 with the hen. Thus, the cock is able to take charge of the nest, should anything happen to the hen.

Like most gallinacious chicks, the quail babies leave the nest as soon as they hatch. They can run and peck for food almost at once and fly in just a few days. Their wing feathers begin to sprout almost as soon as they are out of the shell. Their parents care for them devotedly and they quickly learn to respond to the warning calls of the adult birds. One observer tells of coming upon such a covey unexpectedly while descending a woodland path. The parent bird, a cock, flew right at him and fell at his feet, giving the impression of a dying bird, while at the same time whistling the alarm note. The chicks all flew in opposite directions and disappeared in a flash. The reporter says that he could easily have caught the adult bird, but allowed him to escape, when he began clucking to call the chicks to him.

When summer ends, the quail family still stays together, sometimes joining with neighboring families to form a larger covey. Although they do not migrate in the true sense of the word, they do a good deal of traveling in search of food, almost always on foot. However, that does not mean they cannot fly when necessary, and adult birds have been clocked at 28 to 38 miles an hour. When hurtling away from a hunter, they can go even faster—over 40 miles an hour.

At night, quail like to roost in a circle with all the heads facing out. Often they will use the same spot for several nights: under a protecting fir, in a tangle of briers, or an island in a river or pond. Even young chicks have been known to form this circular roost, a protection against enemies and cold alike. A reporter in 1903 tells how this circle is formed. First two birds stand close together and then others join them, the heads always facing out. In this case, by the time the circle was formed, two quail were left out. They ran around the outside of the circle, looking for a place to squeeze in. One finally managed it, but the last one had to jump onto the backs of the others before finding a spot where it could wedge itself between the closely pressed birds. However, all roosting is not done on the ground. A mass of wild grapevines or a bushy tree or even an old apple tree will do equally well.

In the western part of our country, a number of quail species are found, some of them much gaudier than the bobwhite, with unusual plumes and topknots. Along the California coast and up into Oregon we find two related species, the California quail (*Lophortyx californica californica*) and the valley quail (*Lophortyx californica vallicola*). Both these species have a topknot of feathers, a slender decoration that stands erect atop their heads or nods forward as they run. In the last century there were many thousands of these birds which seemingly rose in thunderous flight from every cactus patch or could be seen trotting in long lines along the road. But heavy hunting over the years has decimated their numbers. Hunters today prefer to shoot the eastern bobwhite, because the valley quail has a disconcerting habit of running away on the ground. To present a good target, a bird should be in the air.

California and valley quail are great vegetarians, only about 3 percent of their food being insects. They especially like seeds, adding to that some fruit, grain, and foliage. They go out to feed in the early hours just after sunrise and again an hour or two before sunset. The time between is spent at some drinking spot or resting in the shade. If they find a good feeding spot, they return to it day after day. Except in the nesting season, they travel in flocks. In the old days, such coveys numbered in the hundreds, but today there may be 30 or 40 birds together.

In spring, the birds pair off and the coveys break up. The males

56

Male California quail

give out their mating call and challenge, *ku-kwak!,* and there may be some fighting before ownership of territory and mate is established. The cock is devoted to his individual hen and helps with the selection of the nest site and the building of the nest. When the young are hatched, he helps care for them, alerting them to danger and leading them to the best feeding places.

Like their eastern relatives, the quail of the Pacific Coast lay their eggs in some odd places. They are fond of grape arbors and vine-covered trellises and one instance has been noted where they nested in a dense wisteria some ten feet above the ground. When the babies hatched and the parents called to them, they tumbled out of the nest, slightly stunned when they hit the ground, but soon able to follow their elders into the wild. The tendency to lay in other birds' nests is also observed here. One bird is said to have laid her eggs in the nest of a long-tailed chat, where both birds took turns sitting on them. And another observer reported finding a quail's eggs in the nest of a roadrunner.

In the mountainous sections of our eastern states live other species of quail: the mountain quail (*Oreortyx picta palmeri*) and the related plumed quail (*Oreortyx picta picta*). These birds like higher altitudes and are often found in semiarid regions. The plumed quail is considered the biggest and handsomest of all North American quail. In summer they can be found up to 9,000 feet (2,745 meters) in the mountains although they come down to the 500-foot level (150 meters) to make their nests. These are very shy birds, more often heard than seen. The hen lays fewer eggs

58

Scaled quail

than the valley quail, and in the higher mountains they have only one brood a season, although in the lower foothills they may sometimes have two broods a season.

In our southwestern desert regions lives still another quail species, the Arizona scaled quail (*Callipepla squamata pallida*). It ranges from the Mexican plateau into southern Arizona, New Mexico, and parts of Texas. It makes its home in dry, barren areas where creosote, sagebrush, and mesquite are the prevailing growth. Around the few streams in such regions grow cottonwoods and sycamores and wild grasses. Here the Arizona quail makes its home. It has been popularly named blue quail or white topknot, which gives an idea of its colorful plumage.

The Arizona quail is more terrestrial than other species, usually making its nest on the ground and preferring to run rather than fly when escaping. They go about in coveys except during the nesting season, when the sexes pair off, much as other quail do. They eat more insects than other species of quail—almost a third of their diet. Of the other two-thirds, half is made up of weed seeds. They like sandy tablelands, where they take frequent sand baths and enjoy themselves chasing each other about. They also need good, fresh water and travel considerable distances to find it.

Like the Arizona quail, Gambel's quail (*Lophortyx gambeli gambeli*) also inhabits desert regions. It can be found from southeastern California through New Mexico, Texas, and Arizona to northwestern Mexico. Its life-style is much like that of its relatives, living in coveys throughout the year except during the nesting season, when it forms pairs. At this time the cocks are as pugnacious as ever and as tenderly attentive to their mates and chicks. They seem to eat far fewer insects than the Arizona quail, which inhabits much the same areas.

Both these desert dwellers face the same enemies. In addition to the human hunter and the wild canines and predatory birds, they must elude the desert animals: rattlesnakes, skunks, and that

60

Female Gambel's quail

big lizard of our southwestern deserts, the Gila monster.

There are numerous quail species native to the Old World. They are the only true migrants among the gallinacious birds. They have long, pointed wings and are good fliers. Seven species are listed: the European quail, the Ussuri quail, the Japanese quail, the African quail, the rain quail, the New Zealand quail, and the harlequin quail. The last is found in Africa and is especially colorful.

The common European quail (*Coturnix coturnix*) is especially interesting because of its migrations. The routes are very complicated, crossing the Mediterranean Sea from France and Russia to

Sicily, Sardinia, and North Africa. Some quail breed in North Africa, but almost as soon as the chicks are hatched, they fly north across the sea, because at that time, in April to June, drought begins in North Africa.

In ancient times, these birds were extremely numerous, and their arrival in the Sinai is noted in the Bible, which tells of the birds coming in great flocks, exhausted by their long journey across water and easy to catch for food.

The African quail (*Coturnix coturnix africana*) moves from one grassy area in South Africa to another, never staying long in one place. It is fond of grain and also eats beetles and other insects. Its call sounds like "*kwot-kwot*" and it usually goes about in pairs. They have a habit of jumping up when disturbed, flying parallel for a short distance, and then crossing over. Sportsmen, observing this, sometimes wait until the birds cross and then bring down both with one shot.

Living in the more tropical parts of Africa is the harlequin quail (*Coturnix delegorguei*). Like its southern cousin, it moves about the land, appearing and disappearing mysteriously. These quail have large egg clutches, as many as 10 or 12.

The smallest of all the quail, the Chinese quail (*Excalfactoria chinensis*), lives in Asia. The nine subspecies are spread over India, Sri Lanka, Malaya, Thailand, the Philippines, Sumatra, Celebes, and parts of Australia. They inhabit brushy thickets and marshy grassland and are seldom hunted because they are so small. The male is brightly colored with shiny green-blue body feathers and black-and-white markings under the chin. They live in pairs and the cocks are very aggressive. For this reason, the natives make a practice of training them for cockfighting.

In Japan, the quail has been domesticated. They were first caged as pets in 1595, because of their melodious voices. Today, however, they are also raised for their meat and eggs.

5 Pheasants

Perhaps the most familiar and easily observed of the chickenlike birds in our northern states is the pheasant. It is often seen running along the road and does not seem as shy as other wildlife. It may surprise some to realize that this spectacle has only been possible during the last hundred years. For the pheasant is not a native American. Much money and a great deal of effort were expended before the introduction of the pheasant was assured and there were many disappointments along the way.

Pheasants are some of the most beautiful of the gallinaceous birds, so it is no wonder that bird fanciers wanted to bring them to America—in fact, to wherever the breeder might be going to live, for they have been carried all over the world from their original home in China. They are very good eating and an exciting bird to hunt.

It is nice to imagine that the first pheasant to be imported anywhere came back with the ancient Greek Argonauts, when they

Male ring-necked pheasant

returned from their expedition to find the Golden Fleece. In addition to bringing back the Fleece and the Princess Medea as wife to Jason, they brought some beautiful chickenlike birds. The word pheasant comes from the Greek *phasianos*, which means a native of Phasis. Phasis was an area of ancient Colchis, and the land of the Golden Fleece, and the birds must have been carried along the trade routes between the two countries. Colchis is now known as Georgia, a part of the Soviet Union and the two ancient names are reflected in the scientific name of the ring-necked pheasant: *Phasianus colchicus torquatus.*

65

Pheasant are native to Asia: China, Japan, and various countries north and west of the Himalayas. But beginning with the introduction into Greece, they gradually spread all over Europe. They were highly valued by the Romans for their elaborate banquets and the Emperor Heliogabalus had his lions fed on pheasants. During the Middle Ages, pheasants were the privilege of royal courts and monasteries. By the year 1050, they were well known in England, and by 1100, the Abbot of Amesbury was asking permission to hunt pheasants. By the sixteenth and seventeenth centuries, pheasant hunting was so popular that it became necessary to pass laws for their protection. Today, many European noblemen maintain large pheasantries where the birds are raised in captivity. Whenever the European populations of the birds decline too drastically, they are renewed from these sources. In spite of centuries of breeding, the birds have not become truly domesticated and they take readily to release in the wild.

The early American colonists made several attempts to introduce the pheasant to the eastern states, none of which was successful. One such importer was Benjamin Franklin's son-in-law, Richard Bache, who released some pheasants on his estate in New Jersey. But the birds simply disappeared. It seemed as though the New World was hostile to the Asian pheasant.

Then almost a hundred years later, in 1881, at the other end of the country in Oregon, a man established the first successful colony of pheasants in America. Judge O. N. Denny had been sent to China as consul general for Shanghai. He was so captivated by the beautiful Chinese birds that he determined to bring them to his home in Portland, Oregon. His first shipment suffered from a gale at sea and the birds arrived in poor condition and all of them died. But when he tried again the following year, 26 of his original 30 birds survived the journey and were released in the woods and fields around his home.

This time Judge Denny was successful, and when he returned from his duties in China, he found that pheasants were plentiful in the Willamette Valley. From there they spread out in adjacent regions, and other states, seeing the success of Oregon, clamored to develop their pheasant populations, too. Birds were also brought to the northeastern states from England. Today the pheasant ranges in most of our northern states and in southern Canada all the way across the country. South Dakota, in the middle of the country, has one of the largest populations and is famous for pheasant hunting in the fall. Strangely, they have never been successfully transplanted to our southern states. There is some mystery about this, because they can adapt to a wide range of habitats. They can live at sea level and at high altitudes. They can withstand winter snow and the heat of California's Imperial Valley. So why not our southern states, such as Kentucky? One theory is that they cannot live south of the marks left by the great glaciers. The calcium in the soil—left by the glaciers—has an effect on pheasant eggs. Too much hot weather also is bad for hatching pheasant eggs. The exception to this, Imperial Valley, has a very dry heat.

The ring-necked pheasant is a cross of several Asian species. The white band around the neck, which gives the bird its popular name, came from the true Chinese species (*P. c. torquatus*), whereas the birds that came from England to our East Coast are a mixture of *torquatus* and the European species, possibly imported by the Argonauts from the Black Sea area. Those birds (*P. c. colchicus*) did not have the white band. There is also some Japanese green pheasant (*P. c. versicolor*) in the mix. Thus some of our pheasants will show a wide white band around the neck, some will have only a narrow band, and some no band at all. But they are all fundamentally the same ring-necked pheasant and can interbreed successfully.

The cock pheasant has a gaudy, almost iridescent, plumage of various shades of green, blue, and brown. In the mating season, his face wattles swell and two feather tufts protrude at the back of his head like ears. His tail feathers are long and thin, with a spotted design, and some of his feathers are shaggy and hairlike. He has strong, sharp spurs, which are almost absent in the females. Hens also have the usual mottled brown plumage of gallinacious females because of their need for camouflage while on the nest.

The life-style of the pheasant is similar to other chickenlike birds. The males display and fight for the females but take no part in nest building or raising the young. This is all done by the hen, which usually nests on the ground and is so well camouflaged that she can easily be stepped on. It is also believed that the females and young chicks emit no smell, for hunting dogs have been known to run right past a hen on her nest. In 1928, tests were made with prize-winning dogs, which pointed 12 birds—all males.

Female pheasant on nest

The hen pheasant is another chickenlike bird that lays her eggs in the nests of other birds. Pheasant eggs have been reported in the nests of bobwhites, ruffed and sooty grouse, and even domestic fowl.

Pheasants seem to be more destructive to crops than other gallinacious birds. They eat sprouting corn and kernels from the cob, also tomatoes, beets, peas, and beans. However, they make up for this by their control of many destructive insects: grasshoppers, potato beetles, and even the larvae of such pests as the gypsy moth and tent caterpillars.

A detailed study of pheasants in the wild was made by the Soviet scientists E. V. Koslova and A. J. Tugarinov in Tadjikstan. According to their observations, the ring-necked pheasant cock does not defend an individual territory and is not as aggressive as other gallinacious birds. Their pheasant population numbered about 20 pairs per square kilometer (0.621 miles) and the voices of the cocks varied enough so that the scientists could recognize individuals by their calls.

Each cock, the scientists state, makes a system of paths through his area of about 1,312.4 feet to 1,640.5 feet (400 to 500 meters) in length. In 20 to 30 minutes, the cock can travel over his paths. When he reaches the end of one, he turns about and goes back. Now and then he stops and calls *"keh, keh, keh!"* He whirrs his wings, making a sound that can be heard at a distance. In April, the birds begin to form pairs. Usually, two hens become attached to one cock. They recognize his voice and respond only to him. When a cock is walking with one of his hens, they communicate with soft cooing sounds. Often he stops to offer her a special bit of food. This may lead to mating between the pair. When the hens start nesting, the cock returns to his solitary life, but if he should meet an unmated hen, he will start courting her.

A German ornithologist Oskar Heinroth, who has studied pheasants in captivity, believes they are more intelligent than many birds. A cock that he had raised became "oriented toward the human being." That is, he became "imprinted" on the scientist from birth and was very attached to him. When the cock matured, he courted the scientist and looked upon Heinroth's wife as a rival to be attacked. To test the bird, Heinroth and his wife switched clothing. This at first confused the cock. But after looking carefully at the couple's faces, he again attacked the woman and courted the man. The scientist says that when he tried the same test on a great bustard cock, that bird took no notice of the human faces, but attacked and courted the clothes they were wearing. Later, when the pheasant was placed in a zoo, he recognized his old friend at once, when he came to visit him after some time.

There are many other species of pheasants in Asia. Two of the most beautiful are the golden pheasant (*Chrysolophus pictus*) and Lady Amherst's pheasant (*Chrysolophus amherstiae*). The golden pheasant is very popular in pheasantries, for it is a magnificently colored bird and also has a mild temper, breeds well, and tames easily. Golden pheasants were kept as decorative birds in China for thousands of years and were often the subjects of Chinese art. They were brought to Europe several hundred years ago and George Washington had some at Mount Vernon. Breeders have produced many different types with varied dark or light plumage.

Recent observation in the wilds of western China indicate that their homeland is in lower mountainous regions, in dense, subtropical jungles. They can be found up to 8,202.5 feet (2,500 meters). The cock's red and gold feathers can be seen from quite a distance as he flies across the dark green jungle. But they do not come out of hiding often and the brown-clad hens are even harder to see. However, at courting time, the cocks can be heard as they call in a metallic voice, making a sound like the sharpening of a scythe. This bird is much more cautious and secretive than the ring-necked pheasant and can run very fast to escape detection.

The golden pheasant is believed to be monogamous in nature. While in captivity a cock is usually kept in a cage with several hens, but if they are released into a large park, they will usually form pairs, establish territories, and drive away other birds. These birds can live to a good age. One breeder reports a golden pheasant that lived for 20 years.

The close relative of the golden pheasant, Lady Amherst's pheasant, lives in mountainous regions farther west in China and in southeastern Tibet. It frequents higher altitudes than the golden, between 7,000 and 12,000 feet (2,135 and 3,660 meters). A high mountain ridge separates the habitats of the two species. Lady Amherst's pheasants prefer rocky terrain with dense thickets of bamboo and brushwood, where they eat the shoots of young bamboo. Occasionally they are found in forests. In winter, they form close groups and move down into the valleys to escape the snow. They are not as cautious as the golden pheasants and will sometimes venture into fields in search of food.

Lady Amherst's pheasants were brought to England in 1828, but despite their beautiful plumage they were not as popular as the golden pheasant, for they need much larger space in captivity. Otherwise, the males are apt to kill the females in a kind of "court-ship frenzy." Doubtless, in the wild the hens can escape. The two species are very closely related and can interbreed easily. The Lady Amherst's is equally long-lived, and an Australian breeder reports a cock that was still courting his hens at the age of 21.

In our own country, where the pheasant is an alien bird, it

seems to be displacing one of our well-loved native birds. This often happens when an imported species competes for living space with a native species. In this case, the victim is the greater prairie chicken, whose booming mating dance is so much a part of our prairie springtime. In the state of Illinois, the prairie chicken population has dropped from several million to a mere 300.

It was at first thought that the decline of the prairie chicken was due to the increasing loss of prairie habitat, as the growing human population expanded into that area. (The pheasant can adapt to a variety of habitats.) But scientists of the Illinois Natural History Survey have learned that the pheasant actively pursues and harasses the prairie chicken, which is a much smaller bird. The frightened chickens hesitate to nest and when they do, the pheasants often lay their eggs in the same nest. Since pheasant eggs hatch several days sooner than those of the greater prairie chicken, the early arrival of the pheasant chicks disturbs the parent birds. They abandon their nests before their own eggs have hatched.

There are still large populations of prairie chickens in other western states, but it is easy to see that if the events in Illinois are repeated further west, the prairie chicken may before long become extinct. Much as the pheasant is valued by hunters, it would be a sad thing to lose our unique prairie chicken. Wildlife scientists are now working to develop ways and methods to preserve the prairie chicken without detriment to the pheasant.

6 Southern Relatives

Because South America was for millions of years an island continent, cut off by the sea from the lands to the north, its flora and fauna are very different from ours. It has been the home of many strange and monstrous animals, some of them extinct, but many still living in the jungles of the Amazon and the pampas of the southern regions. Of course, birds can fly over oceans, and many of our beautiful summer birds spend the winter in the continent to the south. But chickenlike birds do not fly that well. They spend their time walking on the ground in search of food. The only gallinacious birds that migrate over water are the European quails. Thus, South America possesses some of the odder types of galliformes.

One of these unusual birds is the chachalaca, a member of the family Cracidae, another group of gallinaceous birds. Sometimes referred to as Mexican turkeys, they replace the European pheasants and related birds in South America. They have long legs and tails, rounded wings, and well-developed hind toes. Their feathers are usually black or red or olive brown. Often they are marked with white feathers which sometimes make a large crest on the head.

Chachalacas like dense forests and thickets and spend as much time in the trees as on the ground. In fact, they build their nests in the trees, in contrast to their northern cousins, which usually nest on the ground. They are largely vegetarian, but also eat insects and small animals. They walk about skillfully in the top, thin branches of trees and roost in trees at night. The birds seem to prefer gliding to flying. If they wish to move from tree to tree or across a clearing, they first mount, by jumping from branch to branch, to the top of their tree, and then launch themselves into space, gliding on open wings to a lower branch of their destination tree. Only if their goal is too far, or if they are trying to cross an open glade, will they beat their wings and rise to another height.

The chachalaca (*Ortalis vetula*) gets its name from its morning call, which is said to sound like "*cha-cha-lack, cha-cha-lack!*" In early morning, the neighboring flocks join in a sunrise chorus that can be heard all over the jungle. Bright moonlight will also bring on a series of calls. Some singers have softer voices with a higher pitch, possibly the hens. But although they make themselves heard throughout their range, they are shy birds, seldom seen and hard to find.

Chachalacas can be found in one small corner of the United States: the lower Rio Grande Valley in Texas. Otherwise, to see

Chachalaca

them one must go to Mexico and such countries as Venezuela, Costa Rica, Nicaragua, Colombia, or Honduras.

When courting, the male perches in the top of a tall tree and gives forth his cry of *"Cha-cha-lack!"* Presently, he receives an answer from another perching male and soon a number of them

76

are trying to outshout each other. Sometimes a hen will climb up into the tree and sit just below the male, answering him in a softer voice. When the male gets tired of this, he hops down to the ground, where he continues to show off to the hen by strutting and less noisy displays.

If another cock approaches, he is driven away. One observer states that there are usually two hens with one cock, which did not surprise him, for having raised chachalaca chicks from the egg, he found that the hatch usually comprises two females for every male. Cocks fight a lot during courtship. As they have no spurs, they use beaks and wings and feet, and jump over each other in order to peck at the enemy's back. At this season, males often appear with most of their neck feathers missing.

Nest building starts soon after courtship, and the male is said to help the females. Nests are usually in a tree, 5 to 15 feet (1.5 to 7.6 meters) above the ground. It is located near water and bushes that produce the berries that the young birds are fed. Two or three eggs make the clutch, an unusually small number for gallinacious birds.

The chicks leave the nest as soon as their down is dry. The mother usually carries them down, one at a time, with the baby clinging to her legs. This odd behavior has been proved by scientists who hatched chachalaca eggs under a hen. When they raised the hen off the nest to inspect the brood, they found a few of the chicks clinging to her legs. Another time, the same observer watched a hen chachalaca, in a rainstorm, carry her three chicks, one at a time, up into a tree, where she left them perched in a row on a branch 15 feet (4.57 meters) up. Wing feathers grow quickly on the fledglings and in a few days they can fly short distances. Another observer reports watching a chachalaca hen leading three chicks along the ground, while other adult birds were hopping about in the trees overhead. When the observer came too close, the mother bird carried her babies up into a tree and left them sitting on a limb 16.4 feet (5 meters) above the ground. When only a few days old, such young birds may join a flock, dispensing with individual adult care.

All the South American chickenlike birds have a very slow rate of reproduction and are today in danger of extinction unless protected by law. One reason is the small clutch of only two or three eggs. Also young birds do not reach the age of reproduction until two years old and apparently breed only once a year.

Although they are shy in the wild and hard to observe, they are easy to tame and the natives often keep them as pets. However, it is easy to see why they are no substitute for the Old World chicken as a food source. Three eggs a year would hardly feed a family. Nevertheless, they make interesting pets. They become tame and more friendly than the domestic chicken and are said to be more intelligent. There is a report of a chachalaca living in Ocos on the Pacific Coast that was allowed the run of the village. It took upon itself the task of keeping peace among the domestic chickens. If two cocks began to fight, the chachalaca would run up and separate them. It had no trouble enforcing its will. As soon as it appeared, the cocks, apparently aware of the attack they could expect, ran off in different directions. The chachalaca never pursued. It was content with keeping the peace.

An even stranger South American relative of the chicken is the hoatzin (*Opisthocomos hoazin*). Although only distantly related to our chickens, it is usually classed with the gallinacious birds and is a good example of the incredible things nature can evolve when an area is closed off from the rest of the world. The hoatzin is one of the weirdest creatures to be found in South America.

In general, the birds look much like the other gallinacious fowl of the southern continent and like them they live in the trees rather than on the ground. They are about as big as a crow and the sexes are similar, with a long neck and a small head, topped by a bristly crest. They have strong legs with four toes on each. The chicks have claws on their wings and are able to crawl about in the branches of trees and bushes. The claws are shed as the chick grows into adulthood, but the adults continue to use their wings like extra legs as they journey through the vegetation and as a consequence their wing feathers become broken and disheveled.

Fossils of hoatzins have been found in the rocks of the Oligocene Age, 40 to 50 million years ago, and the bones are similar to those of the "first bird"—the Archaeopteryx, which also had claws and lived in the Jurassic period, along with the dinosaurs. It is believed that the first birds evolved from reptiles and in fact, there are many things about the hoatzin that seem to suggest a reptile.

79

In addition to having claws on the hatchlings, hoatzins have an unusual digestive system. Most birds have a small crop in which to store food and a large gizzard, where it is "chewed up" before passing into the intestines. The hoatzin reverses this process, having a crop that is 50 times larger than the gizzard. The crop is very muscular with horny ridges and it is there that all the "chewing" takes place. Hoatzins are vegetarians, and after the bird has torn off and swallowed a quantity of leaves, it becomes top heavy. It flies awkwardly and as soon as it perches on a branch, sits down on its rump as though to keep from losing its balance and falling forward. When resting, they are always sitting with the rump resting on a branch, and they have a special hard callous at that spot of their anatomy. They even sleep sitting on the calloused rump.

Hoatzins inhabit the Amazon Valley and the rain forests of northern South America. Their name comes from the old Aztec language and is said to imitate the bird's calls. They are also called "cigana" or gypsy and sometimes "stinkbird" because of their supposedly bad smell. One scientist who studied them identified the odor with the vegetation in the large crop, which he said smelled like manure. However that may be, the smell is a protection to the birds, as they are considered inedible and so seldom hunted. Hoatzins are gregarious and live and nest in flocks. They are very noisy and their loud shrieks, whistles, and hisses easily betray their presence. When they are hungry, the chicks give a shrill whistle and they hiss if in danger. Like other aspects of the hoatzin, the voice seems more reptilian than birdlike.

The nests of hoatzins are always built over water. This is for the protection of the young, for if danger threatens, the chicks jump out of the nest into the water and swim away, using both wings and legs. Then when all is safe again, they use their clawed wings to climb back into the trees and return to the nest. Both male and female build the nest and there are at least two to six pairs nesting together, sometimes even a larger colony. The nest is a simple platform with no lining and often so loosely constructed that the eggs can be seen from below. Only two to five eggs are laid and both parents take part in the incubation.

The babies are almost naked when first hatched but soon grow a coat of sparse down—and then a second such coat. They stay in the nest for 14 days, but can soon climb about in the branches or dive into the water below if danger threatens. While this young, they are fed by the parents, which open their beaks and let the babies poke their heads far down the gullet for partially digested leaves. After a few weeks, the chicks lose their claws and their swimming ability and when adult no longer venture into the water.

Hoatzins are most active in the early morning and late after-noon and rest in the shade of their trees during the tropical mid-day. They also are conspicuous on bright moonlit nights. All the adults are protective of the babies in their group. One observer in

Guiana saw five birds spread their wings as a roof under which the chicks could climb along the branches in safety. The chicks do not grow their tail and wing feathers until they are almost full size.

As these birds feed on very special plants found in the Amazonian rain forests, they are very hard to keep in captivity. Other food does not agree with them and they wither away. To date, a few months is the longest that they have lived in captivity.

7 *The Incubator Birds*

It has been said that regardless of what extraordinary invention we humans may devise, some creature has already done the job in nature. Thus, a tiny spider was living underwater with air brought down from above long before we invented the diving bell, and the electric eel was using electricity long before Benjamin Franklin and Thomas Edison investigated the phenomenon. And although the incubator for hatching eggs was invented by the ancient Egyptians, several groups of chickenlike birds were already using the technique in southeastern areas of the Old World.

Scientists place the mound-building birds in the same order with pheasants and chickens. In fact, these birds look much like other members of the family, but they have evolved a very different way of incubating their eggs. The hen never sits on her clutch. Instead, the two parent birds, usually working together, build a mound or excavate a hollow in the earth, where the eggs, by various means, are kept at the proper temperature until they hatch.

This family of birds is known as Megapodiidae and they are found in Australia, New Guinea, and some other islands in that region.

There are several different genera and species of mound birds with a variety of popular names: scrub fowl, brush turkey, jungle fowl, mallee fowl. They use various kinds of heat to warm their eggs. If they are living on islands with scant vegetation and large stretches of sand, they use solar power alone by digging into the sand and laying their eggs where the sun will keep them warm. Some birds, living in the interior, use volcanic heat. They dig their nests in soil that is kept warm by underground volcanic activity or even lay them in rock crevices that are warmed by volcanic fires. Birds living in dense tropical jungles, where sunlight never penetrates, use the heat of fermentation. They build large mounds of vegetation—leaves, stems, sticks—as much as 39 feet (12 meters) across and 16.4 feet (5 meters) high. As more and more leaves are piled onto the mound, the material inside begins to ferment and creates heat. The hen then digs a tunnel into the mound and lays her egg inside. But before she is allowed to do so, the cock tests the mound to be sure the temperature is right. He does this by poking his beak inside. If it is too hot, he scrapes off some of the covering. If too cold, he adds more layers.

The first word about incubator birds was brought to Europeans in the sixteenth century by a Dominican monk, who returned from Australia with tales of chickenlike birds that laid eggs bigger than themselves in piles of leaves. He was a bit inaccurate about the size of the eggs and nobody believed that a bird could build

Australian News & Information Bureau Photo by Cliff Bottomley

A scrub turkey, one of the mound-building birds of Australia, on its mound in a sanctuary in Victoria

an incubator. When, a couple of hundred years later, people began to colonize Australia, the first settlers thought the mounds were toy castles for children or perhaps grave mounds. Not until 1840 did John Gilbert, a naturalist, dig up a mound and find that what the natives had always said was true. There were eggs in it.

Mound-bird eggs are unusually large. The birds themselves are about the size of our chickens, which lay eggs weighing 1¾ to 2 ounces (50 to 60 grams). But the eggs of mound birds may weigh 6½ ounces (185 grams). They represent 12 percent of the bird's body weight, whereas a chicken's egg is only 4 percent. A variety of predators recognize the value of mound-bird eggs. Foxes (imported from Europe) dig them up and native peoples consider them good eating. On some islands of Polynesia, certain mounds have human "owners" who dig up and take away the megapode eggs.

Until the latter part of this century, few details were known about the habits of the mound-building birds. Then in the mid-1950s, Harry Frith made a seven-year study of the mallee fowl and later wrote a book about it, *The Mallee Fowl* (1962). His careful, detailed study gives a unique picture of the life-cycle of the bird.

The mallee fowl (*Leipoa ocellata*) gets its name from the region of Australia that it inhabits. This is a dry area of scrub, known as the mallee, which receives only 16.7 inches (430 mm.) of rain per year. The chief vegetation is eucalyptus, which is seldom more than 20 feet (8 meters) high. The leaves of the trees, as well as the bark and twigs, seem harsh and dry, quite inappro-

86

Australian News & Information Bureau

Mallee fowl—male left and female at the mound

priate for making a "compost heap." But the mallee fowl manages
successfully with what nature has provided.

Work on the mound starts in April or May—the fall months for
lands below the equator. Sometimes they use an old mound and
sometimes they build a new one. Young birds, starting out for the
first time, are not as adept as the more experienced adults. It takes

practice to do it right. If an old mound is used, the covering of sand is removed and the old leaves and rotting vegetation are dug out. If a new site is used, a deep hollow is dug into the earth. Since winter is the rainy season, the birds work off and on as the rain moistens the soil.

They dig a pit about 10 feet (3 meters) across and 3 feet (1 meter) deep. When it is deep enough, they scratch in any vegetable litter they can find. Soon the ground is denuded for a goodly area around the pit. The winter rain softens the ground and the debris collected in the pit. On light rainy days, the birds work hard, but dry weather or a violent storm cause them to stop work.

When enough vegetation has been piled into the hole, the birds wait until a good, hard rain saturates it and then they dig their egg chamber in the top of the pile. They clear out all the large sticks and fill it with softer materials. All this work has taken until August, but now the vegetable matter in the pit begins to ferment. The birds kick back the sand and dirt that they dug out of the hole in April or May. This more than fills the hole and may be over 3 feet (1 meter) thick. This layer of sand serves to keep the heat of fermentation in and to keep rainwater out. It keeps the compost heap from becoming either too wet or too dry.

Although the female may have helped the male in the building of the mound, once it is time to start laying the eggs, she does no further work and he takes over the entire responsibility for maintaining the right temperature during the long incubation period. He does this by poking his beak into the mound at various spots and at different times of the day. Scientists believe that these birds have some kind of heat-sensing ability, probably in the mouth or on the tongue.

While the male is keeping close watch on the temperature of his incubator, the hen gives all her energies to laying the eggs. She lays them one at a time, with anywhere from 5 to 17 days between. Egg laying begins in September, the Australian springtime. When the hen is ready to lay, she comes to the mound in a hunched up posture and makes a low call. But the cock will not let her begin laying unless he is sure that the mound is at the right temperature. Then he hastens to open up the mound while she sits nearby, making a crooning sound. She may even approach the mound and make a few scratches to hurry him up. Once he has it sufficiently opened, he gives a few grunts and she runs over to inspect his work. Often she is not satisfied with his opening and he has to dig some more. At last, she gets down into the egg chamber and scratches out a nest. The male stands on the rim and the birds croon to each other while she settles down to the business of laying her egg. As the egg is so large, she may sit there gasping for a bit afterwards before walking out of the pit with drooping wings for a rest in the shade. While she rests, the male covers the egg and scratches back the sand he has removed. This work usually takes two or three hours.

Since the average female lays 19 eggs in a season (sometimes as many as 33) with an average of 6.4 days between each laying, she needs 115 days to lay her complete clutch. In addition, it requires at least 50 days for each egg to hatch. Thus there are 5½ months during which the incubator must be carefully monitored by the male. Adding to this the approximately four months that it takes him to build the mound and bring it to the proper temperature, we can see that the male works hard at his mound for most of ten months of the year.

For the other two months, the pair separate and spend their time simply looking for food. They are mainly vegetarian, eating buds and flowers of herbs and seeds of the cassia and acacia shrubs. If they come upon an insect on the ground, they snap it up, but do not seem to make a practice of seeking such food.

Harry Frith was never able to observe a courtship display or to determine how cock and hen get together. But once the tie has been established, it seems to be for life. One pair that he observed stayed together for six years, and six other banded pairs, for at least four or five years. However, the birds are primarily solitary and do not even roost together. This is well demonstrated in the behavior of the chicks.

The devoted care lavished by the parent birds on their incubator and eggs is not continued in their treatment of the hatchlings. The adults seem to have no more interest in their young than certain insects, where there is no relationship between the parents and the offspring. Once the chick has hatched, it is completely on its own. But it is well prepared for this. The large size of the egg and the length of incubation produces a highly developed chick, able to dig itself out of the leaves and sand and run and feed itself almost at once. In fact, its flight feathers, as opposed to its baby down, are so well developed that it can fly within 24 hours and can roost for the night in trees or bushes.

On one occasion, Frith watched the emergence of a baby chick. The male bird was opening the mound so that the female could go in and lay an egg. When he had dug down about a foot, he uncovered a chick that was trying to get out. The cock did not pause in his work. He kicked the chick out along with the sand. The baby rolled down the mound right in front of its mother, but she paid to attention. She was in a hurry to lay another egg. The baby, exhausted by its efforts to get out and by its violent ejection, rested a few moments and then staggered away into the scrub.

Mortality is undoubtedly high among the mallee chicks, but so many eggs are laid that the population has remained stable until recent years. Today, as with so many birds and animals, their numbers are decreasing. The chief villain is loss of habitat, due to continual clearing of the scrub for agricultural purposes. Another reason is the introduction of sheep into the scrub. The animals can drastically reduce the food available to the birds. As a result of Harry Frith's study, a preserve has been set aside to protect the mallee fowl.

All things considered, nature's incubator hardly seems to be an improvement on the usual method of incubating avian eggs. The mallee cock works hard for ten months of the year, building and tending his incubator. And when the hen is not helping him, she is laying eggs so big that the process is painful and exhausting.

Most birds sit on their eggs for a number of weeks and then spend a few more feeding and tending the nestlings. I doubt if this entire regimen can compare with the hard digging that the mound birds put in over most of the year.

Bibliography

Bent, Arthur Cleveland. *Life Histories of North American Gallinaceous Birds.* New York: Dover Publications, Inc., 1932.

Grzimek, Bernhard. *Animal Life Encyclopedia,* vol. 9, Birds. New York: Van Nostrand Reinhold Co., 1972.

Roberts, Austin. *The Birds of South Africa.* London: H. F. & G. Witherby Ltd., 1940.

Rowley, Ian. *Bird Life.* New York: Taplinger Publishing Co., Inc., 1974.

Rue, Leonard Lee, III. *The World of the Ruffed Grouse.* Philadelphia: J. B. Lippincott Company, 1973.

Wood-Gush, D. G. M. "A History of the Domestic Chicken from Antiquity to the 19th Century." *Poultry Science* (1959) 38:321-326.

Index